MARRIAGE AND AGING COUPLES

HOW RELATIONSHIPS EVOLVE AS COUPLES GROW OLDER AND FACE LIFE TRANSITIONS TOGETHER

By

EMMANUEL BISHOP

COPYRIGHT © 2024

2

TABLE OF CONTENTS

INTRODUCTION:

THE JOURNEY OF MARRIAGE THROUGH AGING

Marriage is a journey that spans a lifetime, evolving as couples grow older and face new phases of life together. What starts with youthful passion and excitement often transforms into a deep, enduring partnership built on shared experiences, mutual support, and resilience. As individuals age, so too does their relationship, shifting through different stages each with its own unique challenges and rewards.

In the early years of marriage, couples often focus on building their lives together. They are filled with dreams of the future, setting goals, establishing careers, and sometimes starting a family. This period of life is marked by rapid growth and change, and many couples find that they must constantly adapt to new realities. However, the foundation built during this time often sets the tone for the entire marriage, with trust, communication, and shared values becoming essential elements that sustain the relationship over time.

As couples enter middle age, their roles may begin to shift. The pressures of raising children, managing careers, and navigating personal ambitions often take center stage. Marital dynamics during this period can be complex, as partners juggle the demands of work and family life while seeking to maintain their emotional connection. However, as children grow up and careers stabilize, couples may find themselves entering the "empty nest" stage, a time when they must redefine their relationship without the constant presence of children or the focus on external responsibilities. For many, this stage presents an opportunity to reconnect and explore new ways of being together.

Aging brings both physical and emotional changes that can profoundly affect a marriage. As couples face health concerns, retirement, and the realities of growing older, the relationship often takes on a new dimension. Physical changes can impact intimacy, and emotional shifts may challenge the way partners relate to one another. But with these challenges come new opportunities for deepening the bond. In later life, emotional intimacy often becomes a central focus, as couples lean on one another for support and companionship. The shared history and understanding that comes from decades of being together can strengthen the connection in ways that are both profound and comforting.

For many couples, the aging process also brings a shift in priorities. With careers winding down and children having moved out, couples may have more time to dedicate to one another. This stage of marriage can be a time of renewal, where partners rediscover shared interests, embark on new adventures, or find fulfillment in quieter, more reflective moments together.

However, it can also be a period of adjustment, as partners navigate health issues, financial concerns, and the emotional toll of aging.

One of the most significant aspects of marriage through aging is the role of caregiving. In later years, one partner may take on the role of caregiver if the other faces illness or disability. This shift can be emotionally and physically taxing, but it can also be an opportunity for profound acts of love and dedication. In these moments, the strength of the marital bond is often tested and reinforced, as couples navigate difficult circumstances with grace and empathy.

As couples grow older together, they also confront the reality of mortality. End-of-life discussions, preparing for the inevitable, and facing the loss of loved ones become more prominent. However, many couples find comfort in facing these realities as a team, drawing on their years of shared experience to provide strength and solace to one another.

The journey of marriage through aging is not always easy, but it is one of the most rewarding aspects of a lifelong partnership. As couples evolve together, they learn to embrace change, adapt to new challenges, and find joy in the simple act of being with one another. Growing old together is a testament to the resilience of love, a reminder that the bonds formed in youth can deepen and flourish in the later stages of life. It is through this journey that couples discover the true meaning of commitment, companionship, and enduring love.

THE EARLY YEARS: BUILDING THE FOUNDATION

The early years of marriage are a crucial period when couples begin to establish the foundation of their lifelong partnership. This time is often filled with excitement, new experiences, and the joy of creating a life together. However, it is also a time when couples lay the groundwork for how they will navigate challenges, build trust, and form a lasting bond. The decisions, habits, and dynamics that take shape during these early years will often influence the course of the marriage for decades to come.

In the beginning, the excitement of being newly married can make everything seem possible. Couples are typically in the honeymoon phase, where love, passion, and optimism are at their peak. There is a sense of discovery, as partners learn more about each other's habits, values, and dreams. It's a time of deep emotional and physical connection, where building intimacy and trust happens naturally.

However, even during these blissful early stages, couples are also faced with the realities of blending two lives. Adjusting to living together, managing household responsibilities, and navigating different communication styles are key challenges. While love and attraction may initially drive the relationship, practical aspects such as shared decision-making, financial management, and division of household chores quickly come to the forefront.

Communication is one of the most important skills that couples develop in the early years. Establishing open, honest, and respectful communication helps lay a strong foundation for resolving conflicts, expressing needs, and fostering emotional intimacy. Learning how to listen to one another, show empathy, and handle disagreements constructively is essential to maintaining harmony and avoiding long-term resentment.

Trust is another cornerstone of the early years of marriage. Trust is built through small, everyday acts of consistency, honesty, and reliability. Whether it's following through on commitments, being honest about finances, or offering emotional support during stressful times, each partner's actions help build a sense of security and reliability. Trust creates a safe space in the marriage, where both partners feel they can be vulnerable without fear of judgment or betrayal.

Another key aspect of the early years is defining and negotiating shared goals and values. This often involves discussions about family, careers, finances, and future plans. While couples may have individual aspirations, aligning their visions for the future helps them move forward as a unified team. Topics such as whether to have children, career ambitions, lifestyle preferences, and financial priorities are often decided during these foundational years. Compromise and flexibility are crucial in ensuring that both partners feel heard and respected in shaping their future together.

Financial management is a common source of stress in the early stages of marriage. Whether a couple is wealthy or just starting out, money matters can affect the relationship. Discussing and agreeing on budgeting, spending habits, and financial goals is vital to avoid conflicts down the road. Some couples merge their finances, while others maintain separate accounts, but the key is mutual agreement on how to handle their financial future.

Balancing individuality and togetherness is another challenge that arises during the early years. While marriage brings two people closer, it's important for both partners to maintain their sense of self. Healthy relationships allow space for personal growth, hobbies, and friendships outside the marriage. Maintaining individuality within the partnership fosters respect, reduces dependency, and keeps the relationship fresh and dynamic.

Conflict resolution during the early years sets the tone for how couples will handle disagreements throughout their marriage. Differences of opinion are inevitable, but how these conflicts are addressed determines whether they strengthen or weaken the relationship. Learning to compromise, finding common ground, and resolving issues respectfully without blaming or attacking one another are skills that couples develop during this period.

Building a strong foundation in the early years also involves nurturing emotional intimacy. Beyond physical attraction, emotional closeness grows as couples learn to understand each other's deeper needs, fears, and desires. Sharing vulnerabilities, offering support, and celebrating each other's successes creates a bond that goes beyond the initial stages of love. Couples who invest in emotional intimacy from the start are more likely to weather the storms of life with resilience.

While the early years are filled with opportunities for growth and connection, they also require intentional effort and commitment. Establishing a solid foundation doesn't happen by accident; it involves conscious decisions, active listening, and working together toward a shared vision of the future. Couples who prioritize communication, trust, shared values, and emotional intimacy during this time are setting themselves up for long-term success.

As the early years of marriage transition into the middle stages, the foundation built during this period will provide the stability needed to navigate future challenges. Whether it's facing financial difficulties, raising children, or managing career changes, couples who have invested in their relationship during the early years will find that they have the strength and resilience to handle whatever comes their way.

In conclusion, the early years of marriage are a time of building, learning, and growing together. By focusing on communication, trust, shared goals, and emotional connection, couples can lay the groundwork for a fulfilling and lasting partnership. The habits and values formed during this stage will carry them through the inevitable ups and downs of life, ensuring that their marriage remains strong and supportive as they journey through the years together.

MIDLIFE TRANSITIONS: REDEFINING ROLES AND EXPECTATIONS

Midlife is often described as a time of significant change for individuals and couples alike. As people approach their **40s** and **50s**, they often experience transitions that challenge the roles, responsibilities, and expectations they've developed over the years. These changes, both internal and external, can impact the dynamics of a marriage, requiring partners to adjust, redefine their roles, and reassess what they want from their relationship.

During the midlife stage, many couples are well-established in their careers and family life. They've likely spent years juggling the demands of work, raising children, and managing household responsibilities. However, this period often brings a shift in priorities and the need to adapt to new realities, including the changing needs of children, shifts in career focus, and evolving personal aspirations. While midlife transitions can be challenging, they also present an opportunity for couples to reconnect, realign, and strengthen their bond.

1::Parenting and the Empty Nest

For many couples, midlife marks a significant change in their role as parents. Children who once required constant attention and care are growing up, becoming more independent, and eventually leaving home. The transition to an "empty nest" can be both liberating and unsettling for couples. On one hand, it offers the chance to focus more on the relationship and personal interests. On the other hand, it can lead to feelings of loss, identity shifts, and the challenge of rediscovering life as a couple without the day-to-day demands of parenting.

Some couples may feel a sense of relief and excitement as they reclaim time for themselves, travel, pursue hobbies, or rediscover activities they once enjoyed before children dominated their schedules. However, for others, the empty nest can highlight gaps in their relationship that were masked by the busy nature of parenting. Partners may realize that they've grown apart over the years or that they haven't invested enough time in maintaining emotional intimacy. This period requires intentional effort to reconnect, rediscover shared goals, and redefine what the marriage looks like without the central role of parenthood.

2: Career Shifts and Financial Adjustments

Midlife often brings about career changes whether they're voluntary or involuntary. Some individuals reach the peak of their careers and begin to scale back, while others may feel unfulfilled and consider a change in direction. For some, midlife means facing job loss, early retirement, or burnout. These career transitions can place strain on a marriage, as financial stability and the balance of roles within the partnership shift.

Couples may need to renegotiate how they manage their finances, especially if one partner steps back from full-time work, pursues a new career, or transitions into retirement. Financial concerns, such as paying off debt, planning for retirement, or supporting aging parents, can become more prominent during midlife. Clear communication and shared decision-making are essential during this stage, as couples work together to adjust their financial goals and expectations.

3: Personal Growth and Self-Discovery

Midlife is also a time when individuals often embark on a journey of self-discovery. With children grown and careers stabilizing or winding down, people may begin to reassess their personal goals, desires, and dreams. For some, this period of introspection leads to new passions, hobbies, or educational pursuits. Others may question their life choices, leading to a desire for personal reinvention.

These individual shifts can sometimes create tension within a marriage, particularly if one partner feels left behind or if their personal growth paths diverge. For instance, one partner might want to take up new hobbies or travel, while the other prefers to stay rooted in familiar routines. Navigating these changes requires patience, understanding, and flexibility, as both partners work to support each other's evolving interests while maintaining a sense of togetherness in the marriage.

4: Physical and Emotional Changes

As couples enter midlife, they begin to experience the natural physical and emotional changes that come with aging. Physical changes, such as menopause, reduced energy levels, and health concerns, can affect intimacy and the way partners relate to each other. Emotional changes, such as midlife crises or the reevaluation of life's meaning and purpose, can create additional stress.

For many couples, maintaining physical intimacy in midlife can be challenging due to hormonal shifts, changes in body image, or health issues. Open and honest communication about these changes is crucial. Couples who discuss their concerns and work together to find new ways to connect emotionally and physically are better equipped to navigate this transition.

On an emotional level, midlife can be a time of heightened vulnerability. Many individuals face the realization of their mortality, which can lead to anxiety, depression, or a desire to make dramatic life changes. Partners need to offer empathy and understanding during this period, helping each other cope with the complex emotions that often accompany midlife.

5: Caring for Aging Parents

In addition to personal and marital transitions, many couples in midlife find themselves in the role of caregivers for aging parents. The responsibility of supporting elderly parents whether emotionally, financially, or physically can place significant stress on a marriage. The demands of caregiving may lead to burnout, strained finances, or reduced time for personal and marital connection.

Couples facing this challenge must work together to set boundaries, delegate caregiving responsibilities, and seek support from extended family or professional services when needed. Ensuring that both partners feel supported and acknowledged in their caregiving roles is key to maintaining a healthy relationship during this time.

6: Reconnecting and Redefining the Marriage

While midlife transitions bring challenges, they also present an opportunity for couples to reconnect and redefine their relationship. With children grown and careers reaching their later stages, couples can focus more on their partnership, rediscover shared interests, and create new memories together. Whether it's through travel, new hobbies, or simply spending more quality time together, midlife offers the chance to deepen emotional intimacy and strengthen the bond that has developed over the years.

For some couples, this is also a time to reassess and renegotiate their expectations within the marriage. Roles that may have been clearly defined earlier such as the primary earner or caregiver may shift as personal circumstances change. A sense of partnership and mutual support becomes increasingly important during this stage, as couples navigate life's transitions together.

In conclusion, midlife is a time of profound change and transformation for many couples. Redefining roles and expectations is a necessary part of navigating this period successfully. While challenges such as empty nests, career shifts, personal growth, and health concerns can place strain on a marriage, they also offer opportunities for renewal, deeper connection, and a more balanced, fulfilling partnership. With open communication, flexibility, and a shared commitment to growth, couples can emerge from midlife transitions with a stronger, more resilient bond.

EMPTY NEST SYNDROME: ADJUSTING TO LIFE AFTER CHILDREN LEAVE

Empty Nest Syndrome refers to the emotional and psychological adjustment that parents go through when their children grow up and leave home. While this transition is a natural part of family life, it can be a significant challenge for many couples, particularly if their identity, routine, and sense of purpose have been closely tied to their roles as parents. After years of focusing on raising children, couples often find themselves at a crossroads, faced with the need to redefine their marriage, their daily lives, and even their sense of self.

The empty nest period can evoke a complex mix of emotions. On one hand, it can be a time of freedom, where couples have the opportunity to rediscover each other and focus on personal interests that were set aside during the busy years of parenting. On the other hand, it can be a time of grief, as parents deal with the loss of the close daily contact and the central role that children played in their lives. Many couples find that this period is a mix of both, requiring careful navigation and emotional resilience.

1: The Emotional Impact of the Empty Nest

For some parents, the departure of their children triggers a deep sense of loss or sadness. The home, once filled with activity and noise, can suddenly feel quiet and empty. This transition can leave parents feeling aimless or unsure of their next steps, as the day-to-day responsibilities of caring for children are no longer present. Mothers and fathers alike may experience grief as they adjust to their new role, and this can lead to feelings of loneliness, depression, or anxiety.

In some cases, Empty Nest Syndrome can also stir up feelings of regret or guilt. Parents may reflect on how they raised their children, questioning whether they spent enough time with them or made the right decisions. They may also experience worry about how their children will cope on their own, especially if the children are moving to a distant location or entering a challenging phase of life, such as college or starting a new career.

For many parents, the transition is also marked by a shift in their identity. Over the years, the role of being a parent becomes central to who they are. When children leave, parents may struggle with the question, "Who am I now?" This loss of identity can be particularly difficult for individuals who devoted most of their time to child-rearing and now must reimagine their purpose and roles in life.

2: The Impact on the Marital Relationship

The empty nest phase can have a significant impact on a marriage. After years of being immersed in the needs and schedules of their children, couples may realize that they've drifted apart. Without the distractions and responsibilities of parenting, they are left to confront their relationship in a new way. For some, this can be an uncomfortable adjustment, particularly if their communication has diminished over the years or if they've grown accustomed to focusing on their children rather than on each other.

However, for many couples, this period also offers an opportunity for renewal. With more time and fewer external demands, couples can reconnect, rediscover shared interests, and focus on their relationship. This can be a time of exploration, where partners find new ways to enjoy each other's company and rekindle the intimacy that may have been put on the back burner during the child-rearing years. Many couples find that the empty nest allows them to experience a new sense of freedom, enabling them to travel, take up new hobbies, or simply spend more quality time together.

3: Reinventing Life Without Children at the Center

One of the key aspects of adjusting to the empty nest is learning to shift the focus from parenting to self-fulfillment. This is a time when both partners can explore personal passions and interests that may have been sidelined while raising a family. Whether it's pursuing a career change, taking up a new hobby, engaging in volunteer work, or investing more time in social connections, this phase offers the chance to rediscover a sense of individuality.

For couples, it's important to strike a balance between nurturing their marriage and maintaining their personal growth. While the newfound time together can strengthen the bond, it's also vital for each partner to pursue their own goals and passions. This independence within the marriage helps both partners feel fulfilled and energized, ultimately contributing to a healthier relationship.

4: Communication and Emotional Support

Open and honest communication is essential for navigating the emotional challenges of the empty nest. Couples need to acknowledge their feelings of loss, loneliness, or even relief, and discuss them with each other. Suppressing emotions or avoiding difficult conversations can lead to resentment or misunderstandings, whereas expressing feelings openly allows couples to support one another during this transition.

In addition to communicating with each other, it can be helpful to reach out to friends, family, or support groups. Connecting with others who are going through or have already gone through the empty nest stage can provide valuable insights and emotional support. Sharing experiences and coping strategies can help normalize the feelings of sadness or uncertainty that often accompany this transition.

5: Rebuilding Emotional and Physical Intimacy

With children out of the house, couples have the opportunity to rebuild emotional and physical intimacy that may have taken a backseat during the busy years of parenting. Intimacy is not only about physical closeness but also about emotional connection—taking the time to talk, share thoughts and feelings, and spend quality time together.

Couples can reignite their romantic connection by planning activities that bring them closer, such as date nights, weekend getaways, or simply spending quiet evenings together. For many, this stage allows them to explore new dimensions of their relationship, rediscovering the aspects of their partner that attracted them in the first place. This can be a period of growth, where couples deepen their bond and foster a renewed sense of appreciation for each other.

6: Finding New Roles as Parents

While the day-to-day responsibilities of parenting may lessen, the role of a parent does not disappear when children leave home it simply changes. Parents often find themselves in the role of advisor or mentor as their children navigate the challenges of adulthood. Maintaining a healthy balance of support and independence is key; while it's important to be available when needed, it's equally crucial to allow grown children the space to make their own judgments and gain knowledge from their encounters.

Some parents also find joy in becoming grandparents, which can offer a new sense of purpose and fulfillment. Grandparenting allows couples to enjoy family life in a new way, without the full-time demands of raising children. It also brings a new dynamic to the marriage, as partners share the experience of watching their family expand and evolve.

Conclusion: Embracing the Empty Nest

While the transition to an empty nest can be emotionally challenging, it also offers a period of renewal, growth, and opportunity. Couples who approach this phase with open communication, a willingness to rediscover each other, and a focus on personal fulfillment often find that it strengthens their relationship and enriches their lives. The empty nest provides the space to reflect on the years spent raising a family and to embrace the next chapter with a sense of excitement and possibility.

By investing in their relationship and supporting each other's individual growth, couples can navigate the empty nest with grace, emerging with a deeper connection and a renewed sense of purpose both as partners and as individuals.

PHYSICAL CHANGES AND THEIR IMPACT ON MARRIAGE

As couples age, they inevitably experience physical changes that can significantly impact their marriage. From hormonal shifts to declining energy levels and emerging health concerns, these changes affect not only individual well-being but also the dynamics of the relationship. The way couples navigate and respond to these changes plays a critical role in maintaining emotional and physical intimacy and in ensuring that the marriage continues to thrive as they grow older together.

1: Hormonal Changes and Their Effects

Hormonal changes, particularly in midlife, are among the most significant physical transitions for both men and women. Women often experience menopause, typically between the ages of 45 and 55, marking the end of their reproductive years. Menopause brings about a variety of physical and emotional symptoms, including hot flashes, night sweats, weight gain, mood swings, and sleep disturbances. One of the most notable impacts of menopause is a decrease in libido due to lower estrogen levels, which can affect sexual desire and responsiveness.

Similarly, men experience a gradual decline in testosterone levels as they age, sometimes referred to as **andropause** or "male menopause." This can result in reduced sexual desire, erectile dysfunction, fatigue, and changes in mood. These hormonal changes can influence both partners' physical intimacy, and if not addressed openly, they can create tension or distance within the marriage.

For couples, this phase requires patience, understanding, and open communication. It's essential for both partners to recognize that these changes are a natural part of aging and to find ways to adjust to them together. Rather than avoiding conversations about the challenges they face, couples should discuss their feelings and explore solutions, such as seeking medical advice, trying hormone replacement therapies, or finding new ways to maintain emotional and physical closeness.

2: Body Image and Self-Esteem

As people age, changes in body appearance and function can lead to shifts in self-esteem and body image. Weight gain, hair loss, wrinkles, and other signs of aging may make individuals feel less attractive or self-conscious about their appearance. These insecurities can affect the way partners feel about themselves and their willingness to engage in intimacy.

For both men and women, maintaining a positive self-image during this time can be challenging, especially in a society that often values youth and physical appearance. Partners may worry that their spouse no longer finds them attractive or desirable, leading to feelings of inadequacy or withdrawal from physical affection.

It's crucial for couples to offer each other reassurance during this stage. Expressing love and admiration for one another, regardless of physical changes, helps maintain emotional intimacy and prevents feelings of rejection or insecurity. Being supportive and understanding of each other's vulnerabilities can strengthen the bond and keep the relationship fulfilling. Additionally, focusing on staying healthy and active together whether through exercise, a balanced diet, or shared hobbies can help both partners feel more confident and energized, contributing to a more positive body image and sense of well-being.

3: Health Conditions and Chronic Illness

With aging comes an increased likelihood of health problems, including chronic conditions such as arthritis, diabetes, heart disease, and high blood pressure. These health challenges can significantly impact a couple's daily life, routines, and relationship dynamics. Health issues may lead to physical limitations, pain, or fatigue, which can affect mobility, energy levels, and the ability to participate in activities the couple once enjoyed.

For the spouse dealing with a health condition, there may be feelings of frustration, fear, or helplessness. The healthy partner may also struggle with emotions of worry, sadness, or a sense of loss, as they watch their loved one face physical limitations. Health issues may also affect physical intimacy, especially if pain or fatigue makes sexual activity difficult.

In these situations, the caregiver role can come into play, with one partner taking on more responsibilities to support the other. While this can create deeper emotional bonds, it can also lead to caregiver stress or burnout if the demands become overwhelming. Balancing caregiving with personal needs and maintaining open lines of communication about each partner's feelings and expectations are essential for managing this transition effectively.

Seeking medical advice and treatment options is also important in managing health issues. Many health conditions have therapies or treatments that can improve quality of life and enable couples to continue enjoying their relationship. Additionally, couples can adapt to new forms of intimacy that don't necessarily rely on physical performance but instead focus on emotional closeness, affection, and companionship.

4: Declining Energy Levels and Lifestyle Adjustments

One of the more subtle but noticeable physical changes that occurs with age is a decline in energy levels. As couples move through their middle and later years, they may find that they tire more easily or need more time to recover after physical activity. This can affect the couple's daily routines, social activities, and even their sex life.

For some, these energy changes can create frustration, particularly if one partner experiences fatigue more intensely than the other. The more active partner may feel that their spouse is no longer as engaged or enthusiastic about shared activities, while the partner with less energy may feel guilty or pressured to keep up.

Couples can address this shift by making lifestyle adjustments that accommodate their changing energy levels. Prioritizing activities that they both enjoy and that align with their current capabilities can ensure that they still have meaningful time together without placing unnecessary strain on either partner. Slowing down and appreciating quieter, more restful moments such as enjoying a walk, spending time in nature, or simply relaxing together can foster closeness without the need for high-energy activities.

5: Intimacy and Sexuality in Later Years

Physical changes related to aging can have a profound impact on intimacy and sexuality. Decreased libido, erectile dysfunction, vaginal dryness, and other age-related issues can make sexual activity more difficult. However, many couples find that with the right approach, their physical intimacy can evolve and even improve in quality as they age.

Aging couples often focus more on emotional intimacy and connection than on sexual performance, which can lead to a more fulfilling relationship. Physical touch, affection, and communication become more central to maintaining closeness. Exploring new ways of being intimate, such as through massage, cuddling, or simply spending more time in each other's presence, can help couples maintain a strong physical connection even if traditional sexual activity becomes less frequent.

It's also important for couples to talk openly about their sexual needs and concerns. For many couples, seeking medical advice whether through hormone replacement therapy, medication for erectile dysfunction, or other treatments can help alleviate some of the physical challenges that come with aging. Sexuality doesn't have to diminish with age; it can simply take on new forms, with an emphasis on emotional closeness and mutual satisfaction.

6: Maintaining Emotional Intimacy Through Physical Changes

While physical changes are inevitable, maintaining emotional intimacy is critical to preserving the strength and health of the marriage. Emotional intimacy goes beyond physical connection and is rooted in shared experiences, trust, vulnerability, and open communication. As couples face physical changes, it's essential that they support each other emotionally, offering understanding, patience, and empathy during challenging times.

Staying emotionally connected requires intentional effort. Making time for meaningful conversations, sharing feelings, and expressing gratitude for one another helps couples navigate the challenges of aging together. By prioritizing emotional closeness, couples can ensure that their bond remains strong even as they encounter physical changes.

Conclusion: Navigating Physical Changes Together

Physical changes are a natural part of aging, and they will inevitably affect every marriage. However, these changes don't have to diminish the quality of the relationship. With open communication, mutual support, and a willingness to adapt, couples can navigate the physical challenges of aging together while maintaining emotional closeness, physical affection, and a deep sense of partnership.

As couples grow older, their relationship can evolve into a richer, more fulfilling experience that transcends the physical and is rooted in a deep, emotional bond. By accepting and embracing these changes with patience and understanding, partners can strengthen their marriage and continue to enjoy a loving, supportive relationship well into their later years.

EMOTIONAL INTIMACY IN LATER YEARS

As couples age, emotional intimacy becomes an increasingly significant part of their relationship. While physical connection may change or diminish over time due to health issues or aging, emotional closeness often deepens, providing a foundation of love, support, and companionship that sustains the marriage. Emotional intimacy in later years is about understanding, connection, and the shared experiences that form a deep bond between partners. It involves open communication, vulnerability, and the mutual support that couples provide each other as they face the joys and challenges of aging together.

The Evolution of Emotional Intimacy
In the early years of marriage, couples often focus on building their life together, raising children, advancing careers, and managing household responsibilities. As life progresses, emotional intimacy may take a backseat to the

practical demands of everyday life. However, in later years, especially after children leave home and careers slow down, couples have the opportunity to reconnect on an emotional level, rediscovering each other in new ways.

The later stages of life provide more time and space for emotional closeness, as partners shift their focus from external obligations to their relationship. This phase allows for deeper conversations, reflections on shared experiences, and a stronger appreciation for one another. For many couples, this can be a time of renewal, where they strengthen their bond and enhance their emotional connection.

1: Communication: The Heart of Emotional Intimacy

Open, honest communication is the foundation of emotional intimacy at any stage of marriage, but it becomes even more crucial in later years. As partners face the physical, emotional, and psychological changes that come with aging, being able to talk about their feelings, fears, and concerns is vital to maintaining a healthy relationship. Effective communication fosters understanding and empathy, allowing each partner to feel heard, valued, and supported.

In later years, couples often experience significant life changes, retirement, health issues, loss of loved ones that can affect their emotional well-being. Discussing these experiences openly helps couples navigate difficult times together, strengthening their bond. This kind of emotional sharing also allows partners to be vulnerable with each other, creating a deeper sense of trust and closeness.

It's important for couples to make time for meaningful conversations, even in the midst of life's challenges. Simple acts like asking about each other's day, sharing thoughts and feelings, and expressing appreciation for one another can go a long way in maintaining emotional intimacy. Additionally, listening attentively and showing empathy during difficult conversations reinforces the emotional connection between partners.

2: Shared Experiences and Memories

One of the most rewarding aspects of growing older together is the wealth of shared experiences and memories that couples accumulate over the years. These shared moments both the joys and the struggles become a source of emotional closeness and connection. Reflecting on the journey they've been on together, whether it's raising children, traveling, or overcoming challenges, can strengthen the bond between partners.

In later years, couples can take time to reminisce about their life together, celebrating milestones and cherishing the memories they've created. These shared memories provide a sense of continuity and remind both partners of the love and commitment that have carried them through the years. Whether it's looking through old photos, revisiting special places, or simply talking about past experiences, these moments can deepen emotional intimacy and reinforce the couple's connection.

3: Companionship and Support

As couples age, companionship often becomes one of the most important aspects of their relationship. The simple act of being present for one another whether it's sharing meals, taking walks, or just spending quiet time together fosters emotional intimacy. Partners become each other's confidants, providing mutual support during life's transitions and challenges.

In later years, many couples experience the loss of friends, family members, or social connections. This makes the bond between partners even more significant, as they become each other's primary source of emotional support. The companionship they provide each other during times of grief, illness, or uncertainty helps both partners feel more secure and less isolated.

This deep companionship often strengthens the emotional intimacy between partners, as they rely on each other not just for practical support but for emotional sustenance as well. Whether it's through offering comfort during difficult times or simply enjoying each other's presence, this emotional support reinforces the couple's connection and helps them navigate the aging process together.

4: Vulnerability and Trust

Emotional intimacy in later years often involves a greater degree of vulnerability. As couples face the challenges of aging whether it's declining health, loss of independence, or changes in physical appearance there is a need for deeper trust and understanding. Being vulnerable with a partner means allowing them to see and support you through your fears, insecurities, and uncertainties.

For many couples, the ability to be vulnerable with each other creates a stronger emotional bond. Sharing feelings of vulnerability can be difficult, but it is also what allows couples to connect on a deeper emotional level. In later years, this openness can lead to more meaningful conversations and a stronger sense of empathy and compassion between partners.

Trust plays a key role in this process. Couples who trust each other feel safe being vulnerable, knowing that their partner will respond with kindness, understanding, and support. This level of emotional security strengthens the marriage, allowing both partners to feel more connected and supported as they age.

5: Emotional Intimacy and Physical Intimacy

While physical intimacy may evolve as couples age, emotional intimacy often becomes more important in maintaining a close and fulfilling relationship. Emotional connection can enhance physical closeness, as partners who feel emotionally supported and understood are more likely to maintain physical affection, even if sexual activity becomes less frequent.

Acts of affection such as holding hands, hugging, or simply sitting close together reinforce the emotional bond between partners. These gestures of love and care are especially meaningful in later years, as they provide comfort and reassurance. Emotional and physical intimacy are interconnected, and nurturing one often leads to a deeper connection in the other.

Dealing with Life Transitions Together

As couples grow older, they face significant life transitions that can affect their emotional well-being. Retirement, the onset of health issues, the loss of parents or peers, and the process of aging itself are all challenges that require emotional resilience and support. Facing these transitions together helps couples maintain emotional intimacy and strengthen their relationship.

Retirement, for example, can be a time of adjustment, as couples learn to navigate a new daily routine without the structure of work. For some, this period can lead to renewed closeness, as they have more time to spend together and pursue shared interests. For others, it can be a time of tension, as they adjust to spending more time in each other's company. Open communication and mutual understanding are essential during this period to ensure that both partners feel fulfilled and connected.

Health issues can also impact emotional intimacy. Chronic illness or physical limitations may create new challenges for the couple, but they also provide an opportunity for partners to demonstrate care and support for one another. By facing these challenges together, couples can deepen their emotional bond and reaffirm their commitment to each other.

Maintaining Emotional Intimacy: Practical Tips

1: Regular Check-Ins: Set aside time to talk about how you're feeling, your concerns, and your joys. Regular conversations help keep the emotional connection strong.

2: Express Gratitude: Show appreciation for each other's presence, support, and love. Simple acts of gratitude go a long way in reinforcing emotional intimacy.

3: Shared Activities: Engage in activities you both enjoy, whether it's a hobby, traveling, or just taking a walk together. Shared experiences enhance emotional closeness.

4: Active Listening: Pay attention to your partner's feelings and thoughts, and respond with empathy. Being a good listener is key to maintaining emotional intimacy.

5: Physical Affection: Continue to express love through physical touch, even if sexual activity becomes less frequent. Holding hands, hugging, and other acts of affection reinforce emotional closeness.

6: Celebrate Your Journey: Take time to reflect on the life you've built together, the challenges you've overcome, and the memories you've created. Celebrating your journey strengthens your bond.

Conclusion: Emotional Intimacy as the Heart of Aging Together

Emotional intimacy is the cornerstone of a fulfilling and supportive marriage in later years. As physical appearance, energy, and abilities change, emotional connection becomes more valuable than ever. Couples who invest in their emotional bond through communication, vulnerability, and mutual support find that their relationship deepens and becomes a source of strength, comfort, and joy as they age. By nurturing emotional intimacy, couples can continue to experience love, companionship, and connection throughout the later stages of their marriage.

THE ROLE OF CAREGIVING IN MARRIAGE

As couples age, the role of caregiving often becomes a central aspect of marriage. While marriage is traditionally seen as a partnership of mutual support and shared experiences, the aging process can bring about health challenges that require one partner to take on the role of caregiver. This transition can significantly alter the dynamics of the relationship, with both rewarding and challenging aspects.

Caregiving in marriage is a reflection of the commitment and love shared between partners, but it also requires patience, resilience, and emotional strength. Understanding how caregiving affects both the caregiver and the care recipient, and finding ways to manage the physical and emotional demands, is essential for maintaining a healthy and balanced relationship.

1: The Increasing Need for Caregiving in Later Years

As couples grow older, the likelihood of one or both partners facing health problems increases. Conditions such as arthritis, Alzheimer's disease, Parkinson's disease, cardiovascular issues, and other age-related illnesses may require one partner to take on a caregiving role. This caregiving can range from assisting with daily tasks such as bathing, dressing, and medication management to providing emotional support and managing more complex medical needs.

In many marriages, caregiving is an extension of the support and love that partners have provided each other throughout their lives. However, the caregiving role often involves a shift in the relationship's dynamic, as one partner assumes greater responsibility for the well-being of the other. This change can create both physical and emotional challenges for the couple, requiring them to navigate new roles and responsibilities.

2: Emotional Impact on the Caregiver

Becoming a caregiver for a spouse can be an emotionally taxing experience. Many caregivers report feelings of stress, anxiety, and even depression as they manage the day-to-day demands of caregiving while also coping with the emotional strain of watching their partner's health decline. Caregivers often face a range of emotions, including grief over the loss of the life they once shared with their spouse and fear about the future.

At the same time, caregiving can also bring a sense of purpose and fulfillment, as the caregiver demonstrates their love and commitment by providing for their partner's needs. Many caregivers find that their relationship deepens as they care for their spouse, and they develop a new appreciation for the bond they share.

It is important for caregivers to acknowledge their feelings and seek support when needed.

Emotional burnout is a real risk, especially if the caregiving responsibilities are overwhelming or long-term. Caregivers should prioritize self-care, including taking breaks, seeking help from family members or professional caregivers, and finding outlets for their emotions through support groups or counseling.

3: Impact on the Care Recipient

For the partner receiving care, the experience can be equally complex. Physical limitations or illness can lead to feelings of frustration, helplessness, or guilt. The care recipient may feel as though they are a burden on their spouse, particularly if they were once the more independent or dominant partner in the relationship. These feelings can create emotional distance or tension within the marriage if not addressed openly.

At the same time, care recipients often experience deep gratitude and appreciation for their spouse's dedication and support. The caregiving process can be an opportunity for partners to reaffirm their love and commitment, despite the difficulties they face. By acknowledging their vulnerability and allowing their spouse to care for them, the care recipient can contribute to the emotional intimacy of the marriage.

Open communication is crucial for both partners during this time. The care recipient should feel comfortable expressing their needs, frustrations, and emotions, while also recognizing the efforts and sacrifices their spouse is making. Likewise, the caregiver should encourage their partner to share their feelings and work together to find a balance that preserves the emotional connection within the relationship.

4: Balancing Caregiving and Marital Roles

One of the most challenging aspects of caregiving in marriage is finding a balance between the roles of caregiver and spouse. The caregiving role often involves tasks that are more clinical in nature such as managing medications, coordinating doctor's visits, or assisting with physical therapy which can sometimes overshadow the emotional and romantic aspects of the marriage.

To maintain the relationship's emotional intimacy, it's important for couples to set aside time to connect as partners, not just as caregiver and care recipient. Small acts of affection, such as holding hands, spending quality time together, or reminiscing about shared memories, can help keep the emotional bond strong even as the caregiving role becomes more prominent.

Caregivers should also be mindful of maintaining their own identity outside of the caregiving role. It can be easy to become consumed by caregiving responsibilities, but it's important to find time for personal interests, social connections, and self-care. This balance helps prevent burnout and ensures that the caregiver can continue to provide support without sacrificing their own well-being.

5: Practical and Emotional Support for Caregivers

Caregiving can be a full-time responsibility, especially if the care recipient's health needs are complex or chronic. To manage the physical and emotional demands of caregiving, many couples benefit from seeking outside help. This can include hiring a professional caregiver for respite care, seeking help from family members, or exploring community resources such as adult day care services or support groups.

It's also essential for caregivers to recognize their own limitations and ask for help when needed. Many caregivers feel a sense of duty to care for their spouse entirely on their own, but this can lead to burnout. Reaching out for assistance whether through professional services or emotional support from friends and family can make a significant difference in the caregiver's well-being.

Emotional support is equally important. Caregivers often experience feelings of isolation or overwhelm, particularly if they are caring for a spouse with a degenerative condition such as Alzheimer's disease. Support groups for caregivers can provide a sense of community and understanding, offering a safe space to share feelings and gain advice from others in similar situations.

6: The Rewards of Caregiving

While caregiving can be demanding, it can also be deeply rewarding. Many caregivers find that the experience strengthens their relationship and deepens their sense of purpose. By caring for their spouse, they demonstrate the profound love and commitment that has defined their marriage. For many couples, caregiving becomes a testament to the vows they made to support one another "in sickness and in health."

The caregiving experience can also foster a sense of personal growth. Caregivers often develop greater patience, resilience, and empathy as they navigate the challenges of providing care. These qualities not only enhance their relationship with their spouse but also contribute to their overall sense of fulfillment and personal strength.

7: Navigating Caregiving with Compassion and Patience

Caregiving in marriage requires patience, compassion, and adaptability. The role of caregiver often involves unexpected challenges, and both partners must be prepared to navigate these changes with understanding and support. Open communication, mutual respect, and a willingness to adjust expectations are key to maintaining a strong emotional connection during this time.

For caregivers, it's important to approach the role with compassion both for their partner and for themselves. Caregiving can be emotionally and physically demanding, and recognizing the limits of what they can do is essential for preserving their own health and well-being.

For care recipients, understanding that accepting help is not a burden, but rather an opportunity for their spouse to show love and care, can alleviate feelings of guilt or helplessness. By approaching caregiving as a shared journey, couples can maintain their connection and continue to support one another through the challenges of aging.

Conclusion: Caregiving as a Reflection of Love and Commitment

The role of caregiving in marriage is both a challenge and a profound expression of love. As couples age, caregiving becomes a part of the shared journey, with one partner stepping up to provide for the other's needs. While this role can be physically and emotionally demanding, it also offers an opportunity to deepen the bond between partners, reinforcing the love, dedication, and trust that has sustained the marriage through the years.

By approaching caregiving with patience, compassion, and a commitment to maintaining emotional intimacy, couples can navigate this new phase of life together. Caregiving, when embraced with an open heart, becomes a testament to the enduring strength of the marriage and the profound connection that binds two lives together.

RETIREMENT: REDEFINING COUPLE TIME

Retirement marks a significant transition in a couple's life, offering a unique opportunity to redefine how they spend time together. After decades of balancing careers, family obligations, and personal pursuits, retirement offers couples the chance to reconnect and focus on each other. However, the shift from structured workdays to open-ended time can bring both excitement and challenges. Successfully navigating this phase requires intention, communication, and flexibility as couples adjust to their new lifestyle and explore new ways to nurture their relationship.

1: The Opportunity to Reconnect
For many couples, retirement provides the gift of time to travel, pursue hobbies, and enjoy each other's company without the constraints of work

or family responsibilities. With children grown and careers concluded, couples can refocus on their relationship, rediscovering the things they enjoyed together early in their marriage. This phase can feel like a "second honeymoon," where partners explore shared interests, build new memories, and develop a stronger emotional connection.

In this phase, many couples also find new ways to communicate and connect. Without the rush of daily routines, they have the space to engage in deeper conversations, reflect on their life together, and discuss their future goals. This intentional reconnection can strengthen emotional intimacy and bring a sense of renewed companionship.

2: Adjusting to Increased Togetherness

While retirement offers an abundance of shared time, this can also be a source of tension for some couples. After years of being accustomed to individual routines and personal space, the sudden increase in togetherness may feel overwhelming. Couples often have to adjust to spending more time in each other's company and renegotiate personal boundaries. The challenge is to find a balance between togetherness and maintaining individual interests.

For example, one partner might expect to spend every day together, while the other may want to continue pursuing hobbies or activities independently. Open communication is essential to avoid misunderstandings and ensure that both partners' needs are met. Discussing how to spend time together, how much space each person requires, and what activities will be shared or pursued individually can prevent unnecessary friction.

3: Exploring New Interests and Hobbies Together

Retirement offers couples the chance to explore new activities that they may not have had time for during their working years. Whether it's traveling, volunteering, taking classes, or learning a new skill together, these shared experiences can bring a sense of excitement and novelty to the relationship. Trying new things together fosters growth and helps couples bond through shared challenges and successes.

Travel is a popular pursuit for many retirees, as it allows couples to explore new destinations and cultures while creating lasting memories. Volunteering together is another way couples can contribute to their community, which can be a fulfilling and purposeful way to spend time in retirement. Additionally, many couples find joy in taking up hobbies like gardening, painting, or cooking, activities that can enhance both individual satisfaction and the couple's bond.

4: Maintaining Individuality in Retirement

While spending time together is important, maintaining individuality in retirement is equally crucial. Couples who successfully navigate retirement often strike a balance between shared activities and independent pursuits. Each partner should have space to follow personal interests, spend time with friends, and engage in hobbies that are meaningful to them. This balance allows both partners to feel fulfilled as individuals, which in turn strengthens the relationship.

Encouraging and supporting each other's individual interests can prevent feelings of resentment or boredom, which can sometimes arise when couples feel overly dependent on each other for entertainment and fulfillment. A healthy mix of togetherness and personal time ensures that both partners continue to grow as individuals while also nurturing their bond as a couple.

5: Reevaluating Financial and Household Responsibilities

Retirement often brings changes in the couple's financial situation, which can influence how they spend their time. With the shift from active income to retirement savings or pensions, couples may need to reassess their financial priorities and discuss how they will manage their household finances moving forward. Whether downsizing, traveling, or planning for long-term care, it's essential for both partners to be involved in financial decision-making to avoid stress or conflict.

In addition to financial discussions, retirement is a time when couples may renegotiate household roles. If one partner was primarily responsible for household duties while the other worked, retirement provides an opportunity to share these tasks more equally. This adjustment can help ensure that both partners feel valued and that there is a sense of fairness in the division of labor.

6: Challenges and Opportunities in Health and Aging

As couples retire, they also confront the realities of aging, including health changes that may affect how they spend their time together. Physical limitations, chronic illness, or other health concerns can alter a couple's plans and require them to adjust their expectations. However, these challenges also provide opportunities for couples to support each other in new ways, strengthening their bond through mutual care and compassion.

Open discussions about health concerns, future care plans, and lifestyle changes are crucial for preparing both partners to face the aging process together. Couples who address these topics proactively are better equipped to manage health-related challenges as they arise.

Conclusion: Embracing the Next Chapter Together

Retirement presents couples with the opportunity to redefine their relationship, explore new interests, and reconnect on a deeper level. While this phase of life comes with its challenges such as adjusting to increased togetherness, navigating health changes, and managing financial concerns it also offers a chance to enjoy life in new ways. By communicating openly, supporting each other's individuality, and making time for shared experiences, couples can embrace this next chapter with a renewed sense of purpose and connection.

FINANCIAL PLANNING FOR AGING COUPLES

Financial planning is a critical component for aging couples, especially as they transition into retirement. With the prospect of longer lifespans, fluctuating health costs, and potential changes in income sources, having a solid financial plan is essential for maintaining stability and ensuring a comfortable lifestyle. This planning encompasses various aspects, including budgeting, investment strategies, estate planning, and health care considerations. By taking a proactive approach to financial planning, couples can navigate the complexities of aging while securing their financial future together.

UNDERSTANDING INCOME SOURCES IN RETIREMENT

One of the first steps in financial planning for aging couples is understanding the various income sources available during retirement. Common sources of retirement income include:

1: Social Security: Many couples rely on Social Security benefits, which can provide a significant portion of their retirement income. Understanding how benefits are calculated, the best time to claim them, and spousal benefits is essential for maximizing these payments.

2: Pensions: If one or both partners have pensions from previous employers, understanding the payout options and the implications for long-term financial health is crucial.

3: Retirement Accounts: 401(k)s, IRAs, and other retirement accounts provide opportunities for tax-advantaged savings. Couples should develop a withdrawal strategy that balances their immediate needs with long-term sustainability.

4::Investment Income: Couples may have investment portfolios that generate income through dividends, interest, or capital gains. Proper asset allocation and risk management are vital in preserving these investments throughout retirement.

5: Annuities:

Some couples may choose to invest in annuities for guaranteed income during retirement. Understanding the terms, fees, and potential drawbacks is critical when considering this option.

CREATING A COMPREHENSIVE BUDGET

Creating a comprehensive budget is essential for aging couples to understand their financial needs and manage their expenses effectively. Key elements of a retirement budget include:

1: **Fixed Expenses**:

These include housing costs (mortgage or rent), utilities, property taxes, insurance premiums, and loan payments.

2: **Variable Expenses:**

These may vary monthly and include groceries, transportation, entertainment, and discretionary spending.

3: Health Care Costs:

Health care can become one of the most significant expenses in retirement. Couples should account for premiums, out-of-pocket costs, and long-term care needs.

4: Emergency Fund:

Setting aside funds for unexpected expenses, such as medical emergencies or home repairs, is essential for maintaining financial stability.

By creating a detailed budget that accounts for these factors, couples can gain a clearer picture of their financial situation and make informed decisions about their spending.

INVESTMENT STRATEGIES FOR RETIREMENT

Investing in retirement requires careful consideration of risk tolerance, time horizon, and income needs. Aging couples should focus on strategies that provide growth while preserving capital. Key investment strategies include:

1: Diversification: A well-diversified portfolio reduces risk and can improve overall returns. Couples should consider a mix of stocks, bonds, real estate, and other assets to balance growth and stability.

2: Income-Generating Investments: As retirement progresses, couples may want to shift their focus toward income-generating investments such as dividend-paying stocks, bonds, and real estate investment trusts (REITs). These investments can provide steady cash flow to support retirement expenses.

3: Adjusting Risk Exposure: As couples age, it's essential to reassess their risk tolerance and adjust their investment strategies accordingly. This may involve gradually shifting from aggressive growth investments to more conservative options that prioritize capital preservation.

4: Regular Portfolio Review: Periodically reviewing and rebalancing the investment portfolio is crucial for ensuring it aligns with changing financial goals, market conditions, and life circumstances.

5: Planning for Health Care Costs
Health care expenses can significantly impact an aging couple's financial plan. Couples should consider the following strategies to manage these costs:

6: Health Insurance Options: Understanding Medicare, supplemental insurance, and long-term care insurance is essential for managing health care expenses. Couples should review their options and enroll in plans that meet their needs.

7: Health Savings Accounts (HSAs): If eligible, couples can contribute to HSAs, which allow for tax-free contributions, growth, and withdrawals for qualified medical expenses. HSAs can be a valuable resource for managing future health care costs.

8: Long-Term Care Planning: Planning for long-term care needs is crucial, as many individuals may require assistance with daily activities in their later years. Couples should explore options for long-term care insurance, in-home care services, or assisted living facilities.

9: Discussing Health Care Preferences: Open conversations about health care preferences and end-of-life wishes can alleviate stress and uncertainty for couples, ensuring that both partners' desires are respected.

10: Estate Planning and Legal Considerations
Estate planning is a vital part of financial planning for aging couples. It ensures that assets are distributed according to their wishes and that important legal decisions are made in advance. Key components of estate planning include:

11: Wills and Trusts: Creating a will or trust outlines how assets will be distributed upon death. Trusts can offer benefits such as avoiding probate and providing for specific conditions.

12: Power of Attorney: Designating a durable power of attorney allows one partner to make financial and legal decisions on behalf of the other if they become incapacitated.

13: Health Care Proxy: Assigning a health care proxy ensures that medical decisions can be made by a trusted individual if one partner cannot communicate their wishes.

14: Beneficiary Designations: Regularly reviewing and updating beneficiary designations on retirement accounts, life insurance policies, and other financial assets is essential to ensure they reflect current intentions.

15: Seeking Professional Guidance

Given the complexities of financial planning for aging couples, seeking guidance from financial advisors, estate planning attorneys, or tax professionals can provide valuable insights and help couples navigate their financial landscape. Professionals can offer tailored advice, help develop comprehensive plans, and assist with the necessary paperwork to ensure a solid financial foundation.

Conclusion: Building a Secure Financial Future Together

Financial planning for aging couples is a multifaceted process that requires careful consideration, open communication, and a proactive approach. By understanding income sources, creating a comprehensive budget, developing investment strategies, planning for health care costs, and addressing estate planning, couples can build a secure financial future together. As they navigate the challenges and opportunities of aging, a well-structured financial plan can provide peace of mind and empower couples to enjoy their retirement years to the fullest.

GENDER ROLES AND AGING

As individuals age, the dynamics of gender roles evolve significantly, impacting relationships, social interactions, and self-identity. Understanding how gender roles influence the aging process is essential for promoting equity, respect, and healthy relationships among older adults. The intersection of gender and aging encompasses various aspects, including caregiving responsibilities, social expectations, health disparities, and the effects of societal norms. By exploring these themes, we can better understand how gender roles shape the experiences of aging individuals and couples.

1: Shifting Caregiving Responsibilities
One of the most significant areas where gender roles manifest in aging is in caregiving responsibilities. Traditionally, women have been viewed as the primary caregivers within families, often taking on the roles of nurturers for children and elderly relatives. As individuals age, these expectations can create disparities in caregiving dynamics.

2: Women as Caregivers: Research shows that older women are more likely to assume caregiving roles for their spouses or elderly family members. This responsibility can lead to physical and emotional strain, impacting their health and well-being. Furthermore, women often juggle caregiving with other responsibilities, such as managing household duties and finances, which can create additional stress.

3: Men's Evolving Roles: While men have traditionally been less involved in caregiving, there is a growing recognition of their roles as caregivers as they age. Many older men are stepping into caregiving positions for their spouses or partners, challenging traditional gender norms. However, societal expectations may still hinder their willingness to embrace these roles fully.

Recognizing and supporting the diverse caregiving responsibilities of both genders is crucial for promoting equity and ensuring that caregivers receive the necessary support and resources.

4: Health Disparities and Gender Norms
Gender roles can significantly influence health outcomes among aging individuals. These disparities often stem from societal expectations, access to healthcare, and differences in coping mechanisms.

5: Women's Health Concerns: Older women may face unique health challenges, including higher rates of chronic illnesses such as arthritis, osteoporosis, and heart disease. Additionally, women tend to live longer than men, leading to increased risks of social isolation, depression, and mental health issues. The traditional gender role of caregiving may also result in women prioritizing others' health over their own, leading to neglect of personal health needs.

6: Men's Health Risks: Older men may experience health issues related to lifestyle choices, such as higher rates of substance abuse and cardiovascular diseases. The societal expectation of masculinity may prevent men from seeking help or discussing emotional and physical health concerns, which can exacerbate health disparities.

Promoting awareness of these gender-based health disparities is essential for developing targeted interventions and ensuring equitable healthcare access for aging individuals.

7: Social Engagement and Gender Dynamics

Social engagement is vital for maintaining well-being and quality of life in older age. However, traditional gender roles can impact how individuals engage socially as they age.

8::Women's Social Networks: Older women often maintain strong social networks, which can provide essential support and companionship. These connections can help mitigate feelings of loneliness and isolation, fostering emotional well-being.

9: Men's Social Isolation: In contrast, older men may face greater challenges in establishing and maintaining social connections. Traditional notions of masculinity may discourage men from seeking social interactions or expressing vulnerability, leading to increased risks of social isolation.

Creating opportunities for social engagement that consider the unique needs and preferences of both genders can help combat isolation and enhance the overall well-being of aging individuals.

10: Redefining Gender Roles in Later Life
As individuals age, they may seek to redefine their gender roles and challenge societal norms. This process can lead to a greater sense of empowerment and fulfillment in later life.

11: Empowerment through Redefinition: Aging provides an opportunity for individuals to explore new identities and roles, regardless of gender. For women, this might mean embracing independence and pursuing personal interests after years of caregiving. For men, it may involve taking on caregiving roles or exploring emotional vulnerability.

12: Challenging Stereotypes: Aging individuals can actively challenge stereotypes associated with gender roles by embracing non-traditional roles and promoting equitable partnerships. This shift can foster healthier relationships and contribute to greater satisfaction and fulfillment in later life.

13: The Importance of Communication and Support

Effective communication and support are crucial for navigating the complexities of gender roles in aging. Couples and families can benefit from open discussions about expectations, responsibilities, and desires as they age.

14: Addressing Expectations: Conversations about caregiving responsibilities, financial planning, and health concerns can help couples understand each other's needs and preferences. Addressing these expectations early on can prevent misunderstandings and promote collaboration.

15: Seeking Support:

Encouraging individuals to seek support from community resources, support groups, and healthcare providers can help them navigate the challenges associated with aging and gender roles. This support can empower individuals to pursue their interests and prioritize their well-being.

Conclusion: Embracing Equity in Aging

Gender roles play a significant role in shaping the experiences of aging individuals and couples. By recognizing the challenges and opportunities that arise from these roles, we can foster greater understanding, compassion, and equity in the aging process. Embracing new definitions of gender roles and promoting open communication can enhance the quality of life for aging individuals and couples, ultimately leading to more fulfilling and meaningful lives in later years. As society continues to evolve, it is essential to challenge stereotypes and embrace the diversity of experiences among aging individuals, creating an inclusive and supportive environment for all.

DEALING WITH LOSS: GRIEF AND MARITAL RESILIENCE

Loss is an inevitable part of life, and it can take many forms be it the death of a loved one, the end of a relationship, or significant life changes like retirement or relocation. For couples, navigating grief together can either strengthen their bond or create fractures in their relationship. Understanding the dynamics of grief and how to cultivate resilience can help couples support each other during difficult times. This discussion will explore the impact of loss on marriages, the grieving process, and strategies for fostering marital resilience.

THE IMPACT OF LOSS ON MARRIAGE

When one partner experiences loss, it often affects both individuals and the relationship as a whole. Grief can manifest in various ways, including emotional distress, withdrawal, anger, and changes in behavior. Some key impacts of loss on marriage include:

1: Emotional Distress:

Grief can lead to a wide range of emotions, such as sadness, anger, confusion, and guilt. Each partner may cope differently, leading to misunderstandings or feelings of isolation.

2: Communication Breakdown:

In times of grief, couples may struggle to communicate effectively. One partner may want to talk about the loss, while the other may prefer to process their emotions quietly. Tension and annoyance can result from this separation

3: Changes in Roles:

The death of a partner or significant life change can shift roles and responsibilities within the marriage. This can lead to feelings of uncertainty as couples navigate their new circumstances.

4: Social Isolation:

Grieving individuals may withdraw from social interactions, leading to increased feelings of loneliness. This withdrawal can impact the couple's social life and create additional strain on the relationship.

5: Diverse Grieving Processes:

Each person has their unique grieving process influenced by personality, past experiences, and cultural factors. These differences can lead to misunderstandings and feelings of frustration if not acknowledged and respected.

UNDERSTANDING THE GRIEVING PROCESS

The grieving process is highly individualized, but it generally involves several stages. Understanding these stages can help couples support each other more effectively:

1: Denial:

In this initial stage, individuals may struggle to accept the reality of the loss. This can manifest as shock, disbelief, or avoidance.

2: Anger:

As reality sets in, feelings of anger and frustration may arise. Partners may direct this anger toward themselves, each other, or the circumstances surrounding the loss.

3: Bargaining:

This stage involves attempting to regain control or change the situation by making deals with oneself or a higher power. Individuals may reflect on "what if" scenarios.

4:Depression:

Feelings of deep sadness and despair can occur as the individual comes to terms with the loss. This stage often involves withdrawal and introspection.

5: Acceptance:

In the final stage, individuals begin to find a way to move forward. Acceptance does not mean forgetting the loss; instead, it involves integrating the loss into one's life and finding new ways to cope.

Understanding these stages can help couples be more empathetic toward each other's experiences and create a supportive environment for healing.

CULTIVATING MARITAL RESILIENCE

While grief can challenge a relationship, it can also be an opportunity for growth and resilience. Couples can cultivate resilience by employing the following strategies:

1: Open Communication:

Encouraging open and honest discussions about grief can help partners understand each other's emotions and needs. Sharing feelings, fears, and memories can create a deeper emotional connection and foster empathy.

2: Active Listening:

Listening without judgment is crucial for validating each other's feelings. Couples should practice active listening, allowing each partner to express their grief without interruption or attempts to "fix" the situation.

3: Establishing Rituals:

Creating rituals to honor the lost loved one can provide a sense of connection and continuity. Whether it's lighting a candle, visiting a special place, or sharing memories, these rituals can help couples bond while remembering their loss.

4: Seeking Support:

Couples should not hesitate to seek external support, whether through therapy, support groups, or trusted friends. Professional guidance can provide valuable coping strategies and facilitate constructive communication.

5: Practicing Patience:

Grieving is not a linear process, and couples must practice patience as they navigate their emotions. It's essential to recognize that feelings may ebb and flow and that healing takes time.

6: Fostering Connection:

Finding ways to connect and engage in activities together can help couples strengthen their bond. Whether it's pursuing a shared hobby, exercising, or simply spending quality time together, fostering connection can provide comfort and joy amidst grief.

7: Strengthening the Relationship Through Loss

While loss can strain a marriage, it can also serve as a catalyst for growth and greater intimacy. Couples who navigate grief together often emerge stronger and more resilient. The experience of supporting one another through a difficult time can deepen their emotional connection and create a shared understanding of life's challenges.

8: Increased Empathy:

Experiencing loss together can foster a greater sense of empathy and compassion between partners. Couples may become more attuned to each other's needs and emotions, creating a stronger foundation for their relationship.

9: Shared Growth:

Working through grief can lead to personal and relational growth. Couples may learn new coping strategies, develop stronger communication skills, and foster a deeper appreciation for each other.

10: Reinforced Commitment:

Navigating loss together can reinforce a sense of commitment and partnership. Couples may recognize the importance of supporting one another through life's challenges, strengthening their bond.

Conclusion: Embracing Resilience Together

Dealing with loss is one of life's most challenging experiences, but it can also be an opportunity for couples to strengthen their relationship. By understanding the grieving process, communicating openly, and cultivating resilience, couples can navigate grief together and emerge with a deeper emotional connection. The journey through loss can be difficult, but it also holds the potential for growth, understanding, and renewed commitment to one another. As couples embrace the complexities of grief, they can foster a resilient partnership that withstands the tests of time and adversity.

SEXUAL INTIMACY AND AGING

Sexual intimacy is an essential aspect of human relationships that contributes significantly to emotional connection, overall well-being, and quality of life. As individuals age, their experiences and perceptions of sexual intimacy may evolve due to physical, emotional, and social changes. Understanding the dynamics of sexual intimacy in later life can help couples maintain healthy, fulfilling sexual relationships while navigating the challenges that aging may bring.

THE IMPORTANCE OF SEXUAL INTIMACY IN LATER LIFE

Sexual intimacy remains significant for many older adults, providing benefits that extend beyond the physical act itself:

1: Emotional Connection:

Sexual intimacy fosters emotional closeness between partners, strengthening their bond and promoting feelings of love and affection. Maintaining this connection can help combat feelings of loneliness and isolation that may accompany aging.

2: Physical Health:

Engaging in sexual activity can have various health benefits, including improved cardiovascular health, enhanced immune function, and reduced stress levels. Sexual intimacy can also contribute to better sleep and overall well-being.

3:Self-Esteem and Body Image:

Positive sexual experiences can boost self-esteem and body image, promoting a sense of vitality and attractiveness. Maintaining a fulfilling sex life can help older adults feel desirable and confident.

4: Quality of Life: For many older adults, sexual intimacy is an integral part of a fulfilling life. It can enhance overall life satisfaction, contributing to emotional and mental health.

CHALLENGES TO SEXUAL INTIMACY IN AGING

While sexual intimacy is important, several factors can pose challenges for older adults:

1: Physical Changes: Aging often brings physical changes that can impact sexual function. For women, hormonal changes associated with menopause can lead to vaginal dryness, decreased libido, and discomfort during intercourse. For men, erectile dysfunction may become more common, affecting sexual performance and confidence.

2: Health Conditions: Chronic health conditions, such as diabetes, heart disease, or arthritis, can impact sexual desire and ability. Medications for these conditions may also have side effects that affect libido and sexual function.

3: Social Stigma: Societal attitudes toward aging and sexuality can create barriers to open discussions about sexual intimacy. Older adults may feel stigmatized or embarrassed discussing their sexual needs or desires, leading to feelings of isolation.

4: Loss and Grief: The loss of a partner can significantly impact an individual's desire for sexual intimacy. Grieving individuals may struggle to engage in sexual activity or form new connections, leading to a diminished sense of intimacy.

5: Changes in Relationship Dynamics:

As couples age, their relationship dynamics may change. Retirement, caregiving responsibilities, and changes in social roles can alter how partners interact and prioritize sexual intimacy.

ENHANCING SEXUAL INTIMACY IN LATER LIFE

Despite the challenges, there are several strategies that couples can adopt to enhance sexual intimacy as they age:

1: Open Communication: Engaging in honest discussions about sexual desires, needs, and concerns is crucial for maintaining intimacy. Couples should feel comfortable discussing changes in their bodies, preferences, and any barriers to intimacy.

2: Exploring Alternatives: Couples may need to explore different ways to express intimacy. This can include focusing on non-penetrative sexual activities, such as kissing, cuddling, or massage, which can foster connection without the pressure of traditional intercourse.

3: Prioritizing Health: Taking care of physical health can improve sexual function and desire.

Regular exercise, a balanced diet, and routine medical check-ups can help address health issues that may impact sexual intimacy.

4: Seeking Professional Help: If couples face persistent challenges related to sexual intimacy, seeking the guidance of healthcare professionals, sex therapists, or counselors can provide valuable insights and support.

5: Embracing New Experiences: Aging can be an opportunity for exploration and experimentation. Couples should feel encouraged to try new things, whether it's exploring new positions, using lubricants to enhance comfort, or incorporating sexual aids.

6: Fostering Emotional Intimacy: Strengthening emotional connections can enhance sexual intimacy. Couples should engage in activities that promote bonding, such as sharing interests, going on dates, or expressing affection in non-sexual ways.

7: Educating Themselves: Understanding the changes that occur during aging and their impact on sexual intimacy can empower couples. Resources such as books, workshops, or online forums can provide valuable information and insights.

THE ROLE OF SOCIETY AND CULTURE

Cultural attitudes towards aging and sexuality can significantly influence how older adults experience sexual intimacy. Challenging age-related stereotypes and promoting positive narratives around sexuality in later life can help foster a more supportive environment for older adults to express their sexual needs and desires.

1: Advocating for Awareness: Public awareness campaigns and educational programs can promote the idea that sexual intimacy is a normal and healthy part of aging. This can help normalize discussions around sexuality and reduce stigma.

2: Creating Supportive Communities: Building supportive communities that recognize and celebrate the sexual rights and desires of older adults can help create an environment where individuals feel comfortable expressing their needs.

3: Healthcare Provider Training: Ensuring that healthcare providers are trained to address sexual health issues among older adults can help facilitate open discussions and provide appropriate care.

Conclusion: Embracing Sexual Intimacy in Aging

Sexual intimacy remains a vital aspect of life for many older adults, contributing to emotional well-being and overall quality of life. While aging can bring challenges to sexual intimacy, couples can navigate these changes through open communication, mutual support, and a willingness to adapt. By embracing sexuality in later life, couples can foster deeper connections, enhance their emotional bond, and enjoy a fulfilling sexual relationship that enriches their lives. As society continues to evolve, promoting positive narratives around aging and sexuality is essential for ensuring that older adults can experience intimacy in all its forms.

MENTAL HEALTH IN AGING MARRIAGES

As couples age, they navigate a unique set of challenges that can significantly impact their mental health and the dynamics of their relationship. Factors such as retirement, health issues, loss of loved ones, and shifting social roles can create stress and strain. However, understanding these challenges and developing strategies to promote mental well-being can lead to stronger, more resilient marriages. This exploration focuses on the importance of mental health in aging marriages, the challenges couples may face, and strategies to enhance mental well-being and relationship satisfaction.

THE IMPORTANCE OF MENTAL HEALTH IN AGING MARRIAGES

Mental health plays a crucial role in the overall quality of life and relationship satisfaction for aging couples. Key reasons why mental health matters in aging marriages include:

1: Emotional Connection: Mental health significantly influences emotional intimacy between partners. A healthy mental state fosters open communication, empathy, and understanding, which are essential for maintaining a strong bond.

2: Coping with Life Changes: Aging often brings significant life transitions, such as retirement or the loss of friends and family members. Couples with good mental health are better equipped to cope with these changes and support each other through difficult times.

3: Conflict Resolution: Healthy mental well-being can improve couples' ability to resolve conflicts constructively. When both partners are mentally well, they are more likely to approach disagreements with patience, empathy, and a willingness to compromise.

4: Quality of Life: A strong mental health foundation contributes to a higher quality of life. Couples who prioritize mental well-being are likely to experience greater life satisfaction, happiness, and fulfillment in their relationship.

CHALLENGES TO MENTAL HEALTH IN AGING MARRIAGES

Aging couples face numerous challenges that can impact their mental health and relationship dynamics:

1: Health Issues: Chronic health conditions and physical limitations can affect mental well-being. Pain, fatigue, and mobility challenges may lead to frustration, anxiety, or depression, impacting the quality of the marriage.

2: Loss and Grief:
The loss of friends, family members, or even pets can lead to profound grief and sadness. Couples may struggle to navigate their grief together, leading to feelings of isolation and emotional distance.

3: Retirement Adjustments:

Transitioning into retirement can bring both opportunities and challenges. Couples may need to redefine their roles, navigate financial changes, and find new ways to spend time together, which can be a source of stress.

4: Social Isolation: Aging individuals may experience increased social isolation due to health issues, mobility limitations, or the loss of social networks. Isolation can lead to feelings of loneliness, anxiety, and depression, which can negatively affect the relationship.

5: Changes in Relationship Dynamics: As couples age, their relationship dynamics may change. Shifts in roles, caregiving responsibilities, and communication patterns can lead to misunderstandings and conflict.

6: Mental Health Disorders: Conditions such as depression, anxiety, or cognitive decline can significantly impact the dynamics of an aging marriage. These disorders may lead to withdrawal, communication difficulties, and altered relationship patterns.

STRATEGIES FOR PROMOTING MENTAL HEALTH IN AGING MARRIAGES

Couples can adopt various strategies to promote mental well-being and enhance their relationship as they age:

1: Open Communication: Encouraging open and honest discussions about mental health, feelings, and concerns can strengthen the emotional connection between partners. Regular check-ins can help partners support each other and address issues proactively.

2: Seeking Professional Support: Couples experiencing significant challenges may benefit from seeking professional support through counseling or therapy. Mental health professionals can provide valuable tools and coping strategies tailored to aging couples.

3: Engaging in Shared Activities:

Finding common interests and engaging in activities together can promote bonding and enhance mental well-being. Whether it's exercising, cooking, gardening, or traveling, shared experiences can create positive memories and strengthen the relationship.

4: Practicing Mindfulness:

Mindfulness practices, such as meditation, yoga, or deep breathing exercises, can help individuals manage stress and enhance emotional well-being. Couples can practice mindfulness together to foster a sense of connection and relaxation.

5:   Maintaining   Social   Connections: Encouraging social interactions and maintaining friendships can combat feelings of isolation. Couples should prioritize spending time with friends and family or engaging in community activities that promote social engagement.

6: Promoting Healthy Lifestyles: Prioritizing physical health through regular exercise, a balanced diet, and sufficient sleep can positively impact mental well-being. Couples can support each other in adopting healthy habits that enhance overall well-being.

7: Encouraging Independence: While it's essential to support each other, encouraging independence can promote mental health. Each partner should pursue individual interests and hobbies, fostering a sense of identity outside the marriage.

8: Practicing Gratitude: Encouraging a culture of gratitude within the marriage can enhance emotional well-being. Couples can take time to express appreciation for each other, reinforcing positive feelings and emotional connection.

NAVIGATING GRIEF TOGETHER

Grief is a natural response to loss, but navigating it as a couple can be challenging. Here are some strategies for dealing with grief together:

1: Acknowledge Individual Grieving Styles: Each partner may have a different grieving process. Understanding and respecting these differences can help couples support each other without judgment.

2: Create Rituals of Remembrance: Engaging in activities that honor the memory of a lost loved one can foster connection. Whether it's lighting a candle, visiting a favorite place, or sharing memories, these rituals can create a sense of shared remembrance.

3: Seek External Support: Joining support groups or engaging with community resources can provide additional outlets for grief processing. These resources can help couples feel less isolated in their grief.

4: Encourage Professional Help: If grief significantly impacts mental health and relationship dynamics, seeking support from a mental health professional can provide valuable coping strategies and guidance.

Conclusion: Prioritizing Mental Health in Aging Marriages

Mental health is a crucial aspect of aging marriages, influencing relationship satisfaction and overall quality of life. By recognizing the challenges that aging brings and implementing strategies to promote mental well-being, couples can navigate the complexities of later life together. Open communication, shared activities, and a commitment to supporting each other's mental health can lead to greater resilience and deeper emotional connections. As couples embrace the journey of aging together, prioritizing mental health can enhance their relationship and foster a fulfilling, meaningful life together.

SPIRITUAL GROWTH AND CONNECTION IN AGING MARRIAGES

Spirituality can play a significant role in the lives of aging couples, serving as a source of comfort, guidance, and connection. As individuals age, they often reflect on their beliefs, values, and the meaning of life, which can deepen their spiritual journey and strengthen their relationship. This exploration focuses on the importance of spiritual growth and connection in aging marriages, the challenges couples may face, and strategies to enhance their spiritual bond.

THE IMPORTANCE OF SPIRITUAL GROWTH IN AGING MARRIAGES

Spiritual growth encompasses the development of one's understanding of life, purpose, and connection to something greater than oneself. In the context of aging marriages, spiritual growth can bring numerous benefits:

1: Enhanced Emotional Resilience: Spirituality can provide a framework for coping with the challenges of aging, such as health issues, loss, and changes in social roles. A strong spiritual foundation can foster hope, meaning, and inner strength during difficult times.

2: Deeper Connection: Shared spiritual beliefs and practices can strengthen the emotional bond between partners. Engaging in spiritual activities together, such as prayer, meditation, or attending religious services, can promote intimacy and mutual understanding.

3: Purpose and Meaning: Spiritual growth can help individuals find purpose and meaning in their lives, especially as they navigate the transitions of aging. Couples who explore their spirituality together can develop a shared sense of purpose, enhancing their relationship.

4: Increased Compassion And Empathy: Spiritual practices often emphasize values such as love, compassion, and forgiveness. As couples deepen their spiritual growth, they may become more empathetic and understanding toward each other, fostering a harmonious relationship.

5: Supportive Community: Engaging in spiritual or religious communities can provide couples with social support and a sense of belonging. These communities can be invaluable resources for emotional support, friendship, and shared experiences.

CHALLENGES TO SPIRITUAL GROWTH IN AGING MARRIAGES

While spiritual growth can enhance aging marriages, couples may encounter several challenges along the way:

1: Differing Beliefs: Partners may hold differing spiritual or religious beliefs, leading to conflicts or misunderstandings. Navigating these differences requires open communication and mutual respect.

2: Life Transitions: Major life changes, such as retirement, relocation, or the loss of loved ones, can disrupt spiritual practices and routines. Couples may find it challenging to maintain their spiritual connection during these transitions.

3: Health Issues: Physical health problems can limit participation in spiritual activities, making it difficult for couples to engage in shared practices that foster spiritual growth.

4: Social Isolation: Aging individuals may experience increased social isolation, particularly if their spiritual or religious community diminishes due to health or mobility issues. This isolation can hinder opportunities for spiritual connection.

5: Existential Questions: As individuals age, they may confront existential questions about life, death, and purpose. These questions can evoke feelings of anxiety or fear, impacting the couple's ability to explore spirituality together.

STRATEGIES FOR FOSTERING SPIRITUAL GROWTH AND CONNECTION

Aging couples can adopt various strategies to nurture their spiritual growth and enhance their connection:

1: Open Dialogue: Encouraging open discussions about spirituality can foster understanding and connection. Couples should feel comfortable sharing their beliefs, values, and experiences without judgment.

2: Shared Spiritual Practices:

Engaging in shared spiritual activities, such as prayer, meditation, or reading spiritual texts, can deepen the emotional bond between partners. These practices can create opportunities for reflection, growth, and connection.

3: Attending Spiritual Gatherings:

Participating in religious services, spiritual retreats, or community events can provide couples with opportunities to connect with like-minded individuals and strengthen their sense of belonging.

4: Exploring Nature:

Spending time in nature can be a powerful way to connect spiritually. Couples can explore parks, gardens, or nature trails, taking time to reflect and appreciate the beauty of the world around them.

5: Volunteering Together:

Engaging in acts of service or volunteering for causes that resonate with both partners can enhance their spiritual connection. Helping others can provide a sense of purpose and fulfillment while fostering gratitude.

6: Creating Rituals: Establishing personal rituals, such as lighting candles, expressing gratitude, or sharing reflections at the end of the day, can enhance spiritual connection and create a sense of continuity in the relationship.

7: Seeking Guidance: Couples may benefit from seeking guidance from spiritual leaders, counselors, or therapists who specialize in spirituality and aging. Professional support can provide valuable insights and resources for spiritual growth.

8: Practicing Forgiveness: Emphasizing forgiveness and letting go of past grievances can create space for spiritual growth. Couples can support each other in this process, fostering a more harmonious relationship.

9: Navigating Spiritual Challenges Together
When faced with challenges to spiritual growth, couples can adopt the following approaches:

10: Respecting Differences: Acknowledging and respecting differing beliefs is crucial. Couples should strive to find common ground and celebrate their unique perspectives, fostering understanding and acceptance.

11: Finding New Practices: If traditional practices become challenging due to health or mobility issues, couples can explore new ways to engage spiritually, such as virtual gatherings, guided meditations, or books on spirituality.

12: Supporting Each Other: Partners should offer emotional support as they navigate existential questions. Encouraging open conversations about fears, hopes, and uncertainties can strengthen their connection.

13: Creating a Spiritual Vision: Couples can work together to create a shared vision of their spiritual journey. Setting goals for spiritual growth and exploring new practices can provide direction and purpose.

Conclusion: Embracing Spiritual Growth Together

Spiritual growth and connection are vital components of aging marriages, providing couples with emotional resilience, deeper intimacy, and a shared sense of purpose. By recognizing the challenges that aging brings and implementing strategies to nurture their spiritual bond, couples can enhance their relationship and navigate the complexities of later life together. Through open communication, shared practices, and mutual support, aging couples can embrace their spiritual journey, fostering a lasting connection that enriches their lives and strengthens their partnership. As they grow together in spirit, they can find meaning, joy, and fulfillment in their shared journey of love and connection.

THE IMPORTANCE OF SOCIAL CONNECTIONS AND FRIENDSHIPS IN AGING MARRIAGES

Social connections and friendships play a vital role in the well-being of aging couples, significantly influencing their mental and emotional health. As individuals age, the dynamics of their relationships evolve, making it essential to understand the importance of nurturing social ties. This exploration highlights the significance of social connections and friendships in aging marriages, the challenges couples may face, and strategies to cultivate and maintain these vital relationships.

THE BENEFITS OF SOCIAL CONNECTIONS AND FRIENDSHIPS

1: Enhanced Emotional Well-Being:

Strong social connections can boost emotional well-being, reducing feelings of loneliness, anxiety, and depression. Positive interactions with friends and family can provide a sense of belonging and support.

2: Improved Physical Health:

Research shows that individuals with strong social ties tend to experience better physical health outcomes. Engaging in social activities can promote a more active lifestyle, reducing the risk of chronic illnesses and enhancing overall vitality.

3: Support During Life Transitions:

Aging often brings significant life transitions, such as retirement, the loss of loved ones, or health challenges. Social connections provide crucial support during these times, offering companionship and understanding.

4: Increased Happiness and Life Satisfaction:

Social interactions contribute to overall happiness and life satisfaction. Sharing experiences with friends and family can create joyful memories and foster a sense of fulfillment.

5: Cognitive Stimulation: Engaging with friends and participating in social activities can stimulate cognitive function and creativity. Social interaction encourages mental engagement, which can help combat cognitive decline.

6: Shared Interests and Activities: Friendships provide opportunities for shared interests and activities, enhancing quality time and deepening emotional connections. Pursuing hobbies together can create lasting memories and strengthen bonds.

CHALLENGES TO SOCIAL CONNECTIONS IN AGING MARRIAGES

While the benefits of social connections are clear, aging couples may encounter challenges in maintaining and nurturing these relationships:

1: Health Issues: Chronic health problems or mobility limitations can hinder participation in social activities, leading to increased isolation and loneliness.

2: Loss of Friends: As individuals age, they may experience the loss of friends or family members, leading to grief and a shrinking social circle. This might generate emotions of loneliness and despair.

3: Relocation: Moving to new areas, such as retirement communities or assisted living facilities, can disrupt established social connections. Adjusting to a new environment can be challenging and isolating.

4: Changing Social Roles: Retirement can shift social roles, leading to changes in how couples interact with friends and family. Couples may need to redefine their social dynamics and find new ways to connect.

5: Technology Barriers: While technology can facilitate connections, some older adults may struggle with digital communication platforms, limiting their ability to stay connected with friends and family.

6: Social Stigma: Societal attitudes towards aging can create stigma, leading some individuals to withdraw from social interactions due to feelings of inadequacy or embarrassment.

STRATEGIES FOR CULTIVATING SOCIAL CONNECTIONS AND FRIENDSHIPS

Aging couples can adopt various strategies to nurture their social connections and maintain friendships:

1: Prioritize Social Activities: Couples should prioritize social interactions by scheduling regular activities with friends or family. This could include hosting gatherings, participating in community events, or joining clubs or organizations that align with their interests.

2: Engage in Group Activities: Joining group classes, such as art, dance, or exercise, can provide opportunities to meet new people and form friendships while engaging in enjoyable activities.

3: Volunteer Together: Volunteering for causes that resonate with both partners can create meaningful social connections and a sense of purpose. It also fosters camaraderie and teamwork between partners.

4: Leverage Technology: Couples can embrace technology to stay connected with friends and family, using video calls, social media, or messaging apps. Learning to use these tools can enhance communication and strengthen relationships.

5: Maintain Existing Friendships: Regularly reaching out to existing friends through phone calls, letters, or visits can help sustain those connections. Being proactive in nurturing friendships is essential.

6: Seek Out New Friendships: Couples can actively seek new friendships by participating in community groups, attending local events, or joining hobby clubs. Being open to new connections can lead to enriching relationships.

7: Encourage Mutual Interests: Engaging in activities that both partners enjoy can create opportunities for bonding and sharing experiences with friends. This can enhance the quality of social interactions.

8: Practice Open Communication:

Couples should communicate openly about their social needs and preferences. Discussing feelings of loneliness or isolation can help partners understand each other's desires for social interaction.

9: The Role of Family in Social Connections

Family relationships also play a significant role in the social lives of aging couples. Maintaining strong connections with children, grandchildren, and extended family can provide emotional support and a sense of belonging. Couples should prioritize family gatherings and create opportunities for meaningful interactions with their loved ones.

Conclusion: Nurturing Social Connections for a Fulfilling Aging Marriage

Social connections and friendships are essential for the well-being of aging couples, providing emotional support, companionship, and opportunities for shared experiences. By recognizing the importance of nurturing these relationships and implementing strategies to maintain social ties, couples can enhance their quality of life and strengthen their marriage. As they navigate the challenges of aging together, prioritizing social connections can foster resilience, joy, and fulfillment, allowing couples to thrive in their later years. By creating a rich tapestry of social interactions, aging couples can enjoy deeper emotional bonds and a more vibrant life together.

MANAGING CHRONIC ILLNESS TOGETHER IN AGING MARRIAGES

Chronic illness can significantly impact both individuals and their relationships, especially in aging marriages. As couples navigate the complexities of health challenges, the dynamics of their partnership may shift, requiring adjustments in roles, communication, and emotional support. This exploration focuses on the importance of managing chronic illness together in aging marriages, the challenges couples may face, and strategies to foster resilience and connection during difficult times.

THE IMPACT OF CHRONIC ILLNESS ON AGING MARRIAGES

Chronic illnesses such as heart disease, diabetes, arthritis, and dementia can have far-reaching effects on a couple's relationship:

1: Emotional Strain: Chronic illness often brings emotional challenges, including anxiety, depression, and frustration. Partners may experience a range of emotions as they navigate the impact of the illness on their lives.

2: Role Reversal: The dynamics of caregiving may shift as one partner becomes the primary caregiver. This role reversal can create feelings of resentment, fatigue, and imbalance in the relationship.

3: Changes in Intimacy: Physical limitations and emotional stressors associated with chronic illness can affect intimacy between partners, leading to feelings of distance or disconnection.

4: Increased Dependency: Chronic illness may lead to increased dependency on one partner for physical, emotional, or financial support. This can place additional stress on the relationship and alter the balance of power.

5: Social Isolation: Couples may experience social isolation due to health issues, limiting their ability to engage in activities they once enjoyed. This isolation can contribute to feelings of loneliness and decreased quality of life.

6: Financial Strain: Managing chronic illness can result in significant medical expenses, leading to financial stress. This strain can create tension within the marriage, as couples navigate budgeting and prioritizing healthcare needs.

STRATEGIES FOR MANAGING CHRONIC ILLNESS TOGETHER

Aging couples can adopt various strategies to effectively manage chronic illness while maintaining a strong and supportive relationship:

1: Open Communication: Encouraging open and honest discussions about health concerns, feelings, and needs is crucial.It is essential for both partners to feel at ease when sharing their thoughts and emotions, free from the concern of being judged.

2: Education and Awareness: Couples should educate themselves about the chronic illness affecting their relationship. Understanding the condition can empower both partners and foster a sense of teamwork in managing it.

3: Setting Realistic Goals: Collaboratively setting realistic health and lifestyle goals can provide structure and direction. Both partners should work together to create achievable plans for managing the illness.

4: Sharing Responsibilities: Balancing caregiving duties is essential to prevent burnout and resentment. Couples should openly discuss roles and responsibilities, allowing both partners to contribute to care in ways that suit their abilities.

5: Prioritizing Self-Care: Each partner should prioritize self-care, recognizing that their health and well-being directly impact the relationship. Engaging in activities that promote mental, emotional, and physical health can enhance resilience.

6: Seeking Support: Couples should not hesitate to seek support from healthcare professionals, counselors, or support groups. Connecting with others facing similar challenges can provide valuable insights and encouragement.

7: Adapting Intimacy: Adjusting expectations around physical intimacy is essential. Couples should explore alternative ways to express love and affection, maintaining emotional connection despite physical limitations.

8: Maintaining Social Connections: Encouraging social interactions with friends and family can combat feelings of isolation. Couples should seek opportunities for shared activities and social engagements, fostering a sense of community.

9: Celebrating Small Wins:

Acknowledging and celebrating small achievements related to health management can boost motivation and strengthen the partnership. Recognizing progress, no matter how minor, fosters a positive outlook.

10: Creating a Support Network:
Building a support network of family, friends, and healthcare professionals can provide additional resources and assistance. This network can help lighten the load and foster a sense of community.

11: Navigating Emotional Challenges
Managing chronic illness can evoke a range of emotional challenges for both partners. Here are some strategies for navigating these emotional hurdles:

12: Encourage Open Dialogue: Allow space for conversations about fears, frustrations, and feelings. Both partners should be willing to listen actively and empathize with each other's experiences.

13: Practice Patience: Chronic illness can lead to frustration and emotional upheaval. Practicing patience with each other and acknowledging the difficulties of the situation can help couples maintain understanding and compassion.

14: Seek Professional Help: If emotional challenges become overwhelming, couples should consider seeking professional support from therapists or counselors specializing in chronic illness and relationship dynamics.

15: Utilize Mindfulness Techniques: Mindfulness practices, such as meditation or deep breathing exercises, can help couples manage stress and enhance emotional regulation. Practicing mindfulness together can foster connection and calm.

16: Create Shared Rituals: Establishing rituals, such as weekly check-ins or shared activities, can provide a sense of stability and connection amidst the challenges of chronic illness.

Conclusion: Strengthening the Bond Through Challenges

Managing chronic illness together can be a challenging yet transformative experience for aging couples. By adopting strategies that prioritize communication, collaboration, and emotional support, couples can navigate the complexities of health challenges while strengthening their bond. Acknowledging the impact of chronic illness on their relationship and proactively seeking ways to support each other fosters resilience and deepens their connection. As they face the journey of aging and health challenges together, couples can emerge with a stronger partnership, enriched by their shared experiences and commitment to one another's well-being.

FACING MORTALITY AS A COUPLE IN AGING MARRIAGES

As couples age, the reality of mortality becomes an inevitable part of their shared journey. This phase can be emotionally challenging, yet it also offers opportunities for deeper connection and understanding. Facing mortality together allows couples to confront fears, express love, and build resilience in their relationship. This exploration delves into the significance of addressing mortality as a couple, the challenges that may arise, and strategies for navigating this profound aspect of aging.

UNDERSTANDING THE SIGNIFICANCE OF FACING MORTALITY TOGETHER

1: Deepening Emotional Connection: Acknowledging mortality can lead to more profound conversations about life, love, and legacy. These discussions often strengthen emotional bonds and promote intimacy as couples share their thoughts and feelings.

2: Encouraging Honest Communication: Facing mortality encourages open and honest communication about fears, desires, and regrets. This transparency can enhance trust and understanding within the relationship.

3: Fostering Shared Values: Conversations about mortality often prompt couples to reflect on their values and priorities. This process can help partners align their goals and deepen their commitment to one another.

4: Creating a Support System: Facing mortality together reinforces the idea of mutual support. Couples can lean on each other during difficult times, providing comfort and reassurance as they navigate the uncertainties of aging.

5: Promoting Mindfulness: Acknowledging mortality can encourage couples to embrace the present moment. This mindfulness can lead to a greater appreciation for each day and the time spent together.

6: Planning for the Future: Discussing mortality can also prompt practical considerations, such as end-of-life planning, financial matters, and healthcare decisions. This proactive approach can alleviate stress and uncertainty in the future.

CHALLENGES COUPLES MAY ENCOUNTER

1: Fear and Anxiety: The thought of mortality can evoke fear and anxiety in both partners. These feelings can create tension in the relationship, making it difficult to communicate openly.

2: Differing Perspectives: Couples may have different attitudes towards aging and death, leading to misunderstandings or conflicts. One partner may be more accepting of mortality, while the other may resist the idea.

3: Grief and Loss: As couples face the reality of mortality, they may also encounter grief and loss, whether from the death of friends or loved ones or the loss of health and vitality.

4: Health Declines: Chronic illness or deteriorating health can amplify fears about mortality, impacting emotional well-being and relationship dynamics.

5: Unresolved Issues: Facing mortality may bring unresolved issues or regrets to the surface, requiring couples to confront difficult emotions and past grievances.

STRATEGIES FOR NAVIGATING MORTALITY TOGETHER

Open and Honest Conversations: Create a safe space for open dialogue about mortality. Encourage discussions about fears, hopes, and desires related to aging and death, allowing both partners to express their feelings.

1: Explore Legacy and Meaning: Engage in conversations about what legacy means to each partner. Discuss values, experiences, and memories that are important to preserve for future generations.

2: Practice Gratitude: Cultivating a practice of gratitude can help couples focus on the positive aspects of their lives together. Regularly reflecting on shared experiences and expressing appreciation for one another can enhance emotional connection.

3: Engage in Meaningful Activities: Spend quality time together doing activities that bring joy and fulfillment. This can include traveling, volunteering, or pursuing shared hobbies helping to create lasting memories.

4: Seek Professional Guidance: If conversations about mortality become overwhelming, couples may benefit from seeking guidance from therapists or counselors specializing in grief and end-of-life issues.

5: Participate in Support Groups: Connecting with others facing similar challenges can provide valuable support and perspective. Couples can join support groups focused on aging, grief, or end-of-life planning.

6: Create Advance Directives: Discussing and planning for end-of-life care can alleviate stress and uncertainty. Creating advance directives together ensures that both partners' wishes are understood and respected.

7: Explore Spirituality and Faith: For some couples, exploring spirituality or faith can provide comfort when facing mortality. Engaging in religious practices or spiritual discussions can foster a sense of peace and connection.

8: Encourage Self-Care: Each partner should prioritize self-care to manage stress and anxiety related to mortality. This includes engaging in physical activity, practicing mindfulness, and maintaining social connections.

9: Celebrate Life Together: Embrace the opportunity to celebrate life together, recognizing that each day is a gift. Create traditions or rituals that honor the relationship and bring joy.

Conclusion: Embracing Mortality as a Shared Journey

Facing mortality together can be a transformative experience for aging couples. By acknowledging the reality of mortality and engaging in open conversations, couples can deepen their emotional connection and create a supportive partnership. While the challenges may be daunting, embracing this journey together can foster resilience, intimacy, and appreciation for the time spent together. As couples navigate the complexities of aging and mortality, they can emerge with a strengthened bond, enriched by their shared experiences, love, and commitment to one another. Ultimately, facing mortality together can inspire a profound sense of purpose and meaning in their lives, allowing couples to cherish each moment and create lasting memories in the time they have.

REINVENTING LIFE AFTER MAJOR LIFE TRANSITIONS IN AGING MARRIAGES

As couples age, they inevitably encounter major life transitions that can significantly alter the landscape of their relationship. These transitions may include retirement, the loss of a loved one, children leaving home, or health changes. While such shifts can be daunting, they also present unique opportunities for reinvention and growth within the marriage. This exploration focuses on the significance of navigating life transitions together, the challenges couples may face, and strategies for successfully reinventing their lives and relationships after these changes.

UNDERSTANDING MAJOR LIFE TRANSITIONS

Major life transitions are significant events that can reshape the dynamics of a marriage. Some common transitions include:

1: Retirement: Transitioning from a structured work life to retirement can lead to identity changes and shifts in daily routines. Couples may need to redefine their roles and discover new ways to engage with each other.

2: Empty Nest Syndrome: As children leave home to pursue their own lives, couples may experience feelings of loss and emptiness. This transition can prompt a reevaluation of their relationship and future together.

3: Health Challenges: Chronic illness or declining health can necessitate adjustments in caregiving roles and emotional support. Couples may face new challenges as they navigate health-related issues together.

4: Loss of a Loved One: The death of a partner or close family member can profoundly impact a couple's emotional landscape, necessitating healing and adjustment to new realities.

5: Relocation: Moving to a new area, whether for health reasons or lifestyle changes, can disrupt established routines and social connections, prompting couples to adapt to unfamiliar environments.

6: Financial Changes: Retirement or significant changes in financial status can alter lifestyle and plans for the future, leading to stress and the need for reassessment.

CHALLENGES COUPLES MAY ENCOUNTER

While major life transitions can lead to opportunities for growth, they also come with challenges that couples must navigate:

1: Emotional Strain: Transitions often bring a range of emotions, including grief, anxiety, and uncertainty. Couples may need to support each other through these emotional upheavals.

2: Identity Changes: Major transitions can lead to shifts in personal identity, particularly during retirement or the loss of a loved one.Couples might find it necessary to reassess and redefine their roles within the relationship.

3: Communication Barriers: Changes in routines and emotions may create communication barriers, making it difficult for partners to express their feelings or needs.

4: Loss of Purpose: As roles change, individuals may struggle with a sense of purpose or fulfillment, impacting overall relationship satisfaction.

5: Increased Dependency: Health challenges may lead to increased dependency on one partner, creating feelings of resentment or imbalance in the relationship.

6: Social Isolation: Transitions, particularly retirement or relocation, can lead to social isolation, affecting the couple's support network and sense of community.

STRATEGIES FOR REINVENTING LIFE AFTER MAJOR LIFE TRANSITIONS

Couples can adopt various strategies to successfully navigate and reinvent their lives after major life transitions:

1: Embrace Open Communication: Encourage honest discussions about feelings, fears, and expectations. Open communication fosters understanding and strengthens the partnership during challenging times.

2: Redefine Roles and Goals: Collaboratively redefine roles within the marriage, particularly during transitions like retirement or empty nesting. Establish shared goals and new ways to support each other.

3: Cultivate New Interests: Explore new hobbies or interests together. Engaging in shared activities can foster connection and create opportunities for personal growth.

4: Establish New Routines: Create new daily routines that align with the changes brought about by the transition. Establishing structure can provide a sense of stability and purpose.

5: Prioritize Quality Time: Spend quality time together, nurturing the emotional connection. This can include date nights, weekend getaways, or simply enjoying shared activities at home.

6: Seek Support: Encourage each other to seek support from friends, family, or professionals. Joining support groups for couples facing similar transitions can provide valuable insights and encouragement.

7: Focus on Self-Care: Each partner should prioritize self-care to manage stress and promote well-being. Engaging in physical activity, practicing mindfulness, and nurturing individual interests can enhance overall resilience.

8: Create a Vision for the Future: Develop a shared vision for the future that reflects both partners' goals and aspirations. This can help create a sense of purpose and direction in the relationship.

9: Practice Gratitude: Cultivating a practice of gratitude can help couples focus on the positives in their lives. Regularly expressing appreciation for each other can strengthen emotional bonds.

10: Be Patient and Flexible: Recognize that adjusting to major life transitions takes time. Couples should practice patience with themselves and each other as they navigate these changes.

Conclusion: Embracing Change as a Catalyst for Growth

Reinventing life after major life transitions can be a transformative experience for aging couples. By approaching these challenges with openness, communication, and a willingness to grow together, couples can emerge stronger and more connected. Acknowledging the difficulties of change while embracing the opportunities for reinvention fosters resilience and deepens the emotional bond within the marriage. As couples navigate the complexities of aging and life's transitions, they can create a fulfilling partnership rooted in love, support, and shared experiences. Ultimately, embracing change can lead to a richer, more meaningful life together, allowing couples to thrive in their later years.

STRENGTHENING THE MARITAL BOND IN THE LATER YEARS

As couples transition into their later years, the marital bond can face unique challenges and opportunities. The aging process brings about various life changes, including health concerns, retirement, and shifts in family dynamics, all of which can impact the relationship. However, this stage of life also presents an opportunity for couples to deepen their connection and reinforce their commitment to one another. This exploration focuses on strategies for strengthening the marital bond in the later years, promoting resilience, intimacy, and joy in the relationship.

UNDERSTANDING THE IMPORTANCE OF A STRONG MARITAL BOND

1: Emotional Support: A strong marital bond provides emotional support, allowing partners to navigate the challenges of aging together. This support is crucial for coping with health issues, loss, and life transitions.

2: Enhanced Communication: Strong relationships foster open communication, enabling couples to express their needs, concerns, and feelings without fear of judgment.Efficient communication plays a crucial role in conflict resolution and enhancing intimacy.

3: Shared Goals and Values: A solid bond encourages couples to align their goals and values, ensuring they work together toward common aspirations and dreams, enriching their shared experience.

4: Resilience: A strong marital bond can enhance resilience, helping couples face life's challenges with unity and strength. This resilience can be particularly important during times of loss or change.

5: Increased Happiness: Research shows that strong marital bonds contribute to overall life satisfaction and happiness. Couples who prioritize their relationship often report higher levels of joy and fulfillment.

STRATEGIES FOR STRENGTHENING THE MARITAL BOND IN LATER YEARS

1: Prioritize Quality Time Together: Make a conscious effort to spend quality time together, engaging in activities that both partners enjoy. Whether it's a regular date night, shared hobbies, or simple walks, quality time nurtures the connection.

2: Practice Open Communication: Encourage open and honest conversations about feelings, experiences, and aspirations. Create an environment where both partners feel safe expressing themselves, fostering trust and intimacy.

3: Engage in Shared Activities: Find new interests or activities to pursue together. This could include volunteering, joining clubs, taking classes, or exploring new hobbies. Engaging in shared pursuits can enhance the sense of partnership and adventure.

4: Cultivate Emotional Intimacy: Focus on emotional connection by discussing feelings, dreams, and memories. Sharing vulnerabilities and personal experiences can deepen emotional intimacy and strengthen the bond.

5: Express Appreciation: Regularly express gratitude and appreciation for one another. Simple gestures, compliments, or thank-you notes can go a long way in reinforcing love and affection.

6: Embrace Change Together: Approach changes and challenges as a team. Embracing change together fosters a sense of unity and partnership, reinforcing the idea that both partners are in it together.

7: Maintain Physical Intimacy: Physical intimacy is essential for maintaining connection. Couples should prioritize affection and explore ways to keep their physical relationship fulfilling and enjoyable, adapting to any physical changes that may arise.

8: Celebrate Milestones: Celebrate anniversaries, birthdays, and other milestones together. Acknowledging these moments can create opportunities for reflection and appreciation for the journey you've shared.

9: Create New Traditions: Establish new traditions that reflect your current life stage. Whether it's a monthly movie night, holiday celebrations, or weekend getaways, creating traditions can enhance the sense of togetherness.

10: Support Each Other's Independence: Encourage each other to pursue individual interests and friendships. Supporting each partner's independence fosters personal growth while enriching the relationship.

11: Seek Professional Guidance if Needed: If challenges arise that are difficult to navigate, consider seeking the support of a marriage counselor or therapist. Professional guidance can help couples address conflicts and strengthen their bond.

12: Explore Spirituality Together: Engaging in spiritual practices or discussions can provide a deeper sense of connection and shared purpose. Whether through religious practices or personal reflection, exploring spirituality can enrich the relationship.

13: Stay Physically Active Together: Engaging in physical activities, whether it's walking, yoga, or dancing, can promote not only physical health but also emotional bonding. Exercise can be a shared goal that fosters teamwork and mutual encouragement.

14: Plan for the Future Together: Discuss future aspirations, dreams, and plans, whether related to travel, living arrangements, or lifestyle changes. Collaboratively envisioning the future can enhance a sense of purpose and connection.

15: Practice Mindfulness Together: Mindfulness practices, such as meditation or deep breathing exercises, can help couples stay present and engaged in the moment. Practicing mindfulness together fosters emotional connection and reduces stress.

Conclusion: Embracing the Journey Together

Strengthening the marital bond in the later years is a rewarding endeavor that requires intentionality, commitment, and love. By prioritizing quality time, open communication, and emotional intimacy, couples can navigate the challenges of aging while enriching their relationship. Embracing change, celebrating milestones, and exploring new experiences together fosters resilience and connection. Ultimately, a strong marital bond enhances not only individual well-being but also the shared journey of life. As couples face the later years together, their love can continue to grow, providing a foundation of support, joy, and fulfillment. Embracing this journey together allows couples to create a meaningful and lasting partnership, filled with cherished memories and shared experiences that define their unique love story.

CONCLUSION:

EMBRACING CHANGE AND GROWING OLD TOGETHER

As couples journey through the later years of life, embracing change becomes an essential aspect of their shared experience. Aging is not merely a passage of time; it is a dynamic process filled with opportunities for growth, reflection, and deeper connection. Navigating the transitions that come with aging such as retirement, health challenges, and shifting family dynamics offers couples a chance to strengthen their bond and reinvent their relationship.

Embracing change involves accepting the realities of aging while maintaining a proactive approach to love and companionship. Couples who prioritize open communication, emotional intimacy, and shared experiences are better equipped to face the challenges that arise. By engaging in quality time together, exploring new interests, and supporting one another through life's ups and downs, partners can cultivate a rich and fulfilling relationship that thrives despite the inevitable changes.

Moreover, growing old together is about fostering resilience and adaptability. Life's transitions may bring moments of uncertainty, but couples who approach these changes as a united front are often able to weather the storms with grace and understanding. This partnership nurtures a sense of security and comfort, reinforcing the idea that both partners are committed to supporting one another through thick and thin.

Celebrating milestones and creating new traditions also play a crucial role in enhancing the marital bond. Acknowledging the journey shared and the memories created fosters appreciation for the love that has endured through the years. Additionally, remaining open to new experiences whether it's travel, hobbies, or spiritual exploration can bring a sense of adventure and excitement to the relationship, allowing couples to continuously discover each other.

Ultimately, embracing change and growing old together is about choosing love every day, despite the challenges that may arise. It's about recognizing that while aging may bring physical changes and emotional trials, it also provides an opportunity to deepen intimacy, understanding, and companionship. As couples navigate this chapter of life, they can draw strength from one another, finding joy in shared laughter, comfort in mutual support, and a profound sense of connection that transcends the years.

In conclusion, growing old together is not just about facing the inevitabilities of life; it is about cherishing the moments, nurturing the love, and creating a legacy that reflects the journey of partnership. By embracing change with open hearts and minds, couples can transform the aging experience into a beautiful testament to their enduring love, a love that grows deeper, richer, and more meaningful with each passing year.